VASTLY
DISCORDANT
REMUNERATIONS

VASTLY
DISCORDANT
REMUNERATIONS

CASE FOR MODESTLY HIGHER
PROGRESSIVE TAXATION

~50% Rate on Top 0.1% of All Incomes
Annual Wealth Tax Phasing Out Inheritance Tax

Dr. A.G. Alias

"Your story is our priority"

LitPrime Solutions
21250 Hawthorne Blvd
Suite 500, Torrance, CA 90503
www.litprime.com
Phone: 1-800-981-9893

Published by LitPrime Solutions: 06/24/2024

ISBN: 979-8-88703-372-3(sc)
ISBN: 979-8-88703-373-0(e)

Library of Congress Control Number: 2024911381

Contents

Preface

This e-book is a shorter version of a book with the same theme, I have been trying to write since 2012. I couldn't finish it to my satisfaction. I then felt I might never finish it. And I suspended my book project in 2022 to focus on this lengthy summary.

There may be some lacunae in this summary, as in the book version, which was the main reason I was reluctant to finish the book.

I always had a habit of squeezing too much information into "a small space," so to speak, which may also come across as discursive display of matters. I am guilty of that. The reader could see such unseemly displays throughout. I can only apologize to the reader. Perhaps, I should have spent far more time in arranging the matter more elaborately, in an orderly manner. I was aware of that, from the beginning. I chose to rectify it by seeking editorial assistance, for which I was willing spend a good deal of money. But I couldn't find a good editor who would work for my needs. I ended up writing in this uncouth way.

If I expanded this material to up to 150,000 or so words, and divided into chapters to make it more appealing, it might have worked. But in the end, my book ended up this way. If the reader would tolerate my discursive display, however uncouth this maybe, most of what I meant to communicate are here in this summary.

My scholarship in economics is quite weak, which was a critical factor for my hesitation to wind up the book. Then my habitual laziness added to the other reasons.

Despite all such deficiencies, I believe a majority of the readers who take the time to read this would agree with my basic arguments. At 88, my memory for names is strikingly impaired. And I would like to publish this before I become *senile*. I would greatly appreciate if the readers would point out, with or without their suggestions, the "errors" and/or disagreements they encounter with this.

I am a retired, Indian American psychiatrist, arrived in the USA in 1971.

I would state, at the outset that most of us do not have a clear grasp of how unfairly the ***current, "Reagan era"*** (from 1981 to date) ***taxation is tilted against low income-groups when the total*** (both direct and indirect) ***taxes are analyzed.***

A glaring, cruel myth is that the rich pay most of the taxes and that the bottom half pays close to nothing, but too many of them undeservedly benefit from too many taxpayer-supported giveaways and subsidies. Unfortunately, the low-income people, as the title hints, make very little money, especially with the pathetic minimum wage, to pay federal income tax, after paying the required payroll tax, which is regressive and fairly hefty sales taxes (see below).

And picking cotton-like many low-paying farm jobs or other jobs involving back-breaking manual labor, pay very little, compared with Wall Street jobs with limited social value.

Many of them earn in the millions; Maria Bartiromo reportedly makes about $10 million a year, while the US Congress members, or the Supreme Court Justices, also desk jobs, with their enormous impact on the society are paid around $300,000 – the rationalization of this disparity is just rubbish, hogwash, I believe.

They ought to be paid $1-2 million a year with plenty of perks, including handsome pensions for Congress members, to have maybe a different crop of Congress members.

To appreciate differently, watch a *CBS-60-minutes* segment to see how easy to "buy" a US Congress member, for a "modest" price, engineered by Jack Abramoff who claimed to have "bought" some 100 Congress members! I would claim, if they were paid $1-2 million a year based on their seniority with plenty of perks, it would be far more difficult to "buy" such a Congress member.

Many Junior Congress members may not realize how "big" their jobs are, whereas, independently wealthy members, like Ted Kennedy or Dianne Feinstein, and exceptionally powerful members like Wilbur Mills, who waited for the right moment to bring President Lyndon Johnson's Medicaid bill for a vote, or Mitch McConnell who gave the current Supreme Court that overturned the 50-year-old Roe v. Wade, did know and appreciate their power and importance.

I grew up in a village in India, but I was not required to do much 0manual labor. When I watched men and women engaging in different kinds of back-breaking manual labor, I felt what they were doing was *real work*. As a physician, I felt I was engaging in "work" only rarely, when I was very busy, which might be less than 10% of the time I was supposedly "working." Now, as a retired State Hospital psychiatrist, I draw handsome pensions from the Sates of Missouri and Illinois, the latter does not even take any State Income Tax, but I have to pay that to the Missouri state treasury.

It's true that money and wealth may not be the *principal* factor that determines our happiness. Nevertheless, once one is devoid of physical and mental pain and discomfort, money can acquire a good deal of happiness.

Others that determine our happiness are *mental* and physical health, association including with the spouse and family, with friends, with relatives, colleagues and with neighbors, as well as age, gender, race/ethnicity, intelligence, looks and plain likeability*.

***Likeability** may largely be inborn. (Likeability and charisma may not be the same but are mutually dependent, I believe) An illustrative example for innate likeability variation is the perceivably *higher likeability (and charisma) of President George W. Bush compared with his father, President George H.W. Bush as well as his brother Governor Jeb Bush*, who ran for president in 2016 - Jeb Bush once even implored his audience, "Please clap!" (This likeability/charisma with at least moderate eloquence are necessary for influencing the masses, such as *for tax-hikes* [e.g., Franklin Roosevelt, in the 1940s] or *for tax-cuts* [e.g., Ronald Reagan, in the 1980s])

Bush_41 (GHWB) was an *underappreciated*, *great* president, often with surprisingly excellent judgments on issues that mattered in the long run. His subdued reaction when the Berlin wall fell and his characteristically restrained prosecution of the first Iraq war, as against Bush_43's (GWB) reckless, disastrous, rather catastrophic invasion of Iraq, in 2003 with the creation of a most brutal ISIS and a long- lasting Sunni-Shia strife there, are illustrative examples. Bush_41 was also conscientious to send troops to Somalia towards relieving famine there, *AFTER* he lost his reelection bid. And Bush_43 as president was among the *worst few*, but he left his presidency minimally scathed, compared with Bill Clinton [!] a "dividend" for his higher likeability, I would argue. (Karl Rove was awestruck when he first met George W Bush. Rove said, "[H]e'd never seen so much charisma in one person in all his life.")

Franklin Delano Roosevelt (FDR), Ronald Reagan, Barack Obama, and John F Kennedy (JFK) are also great examples of innate, high likeability whereas, Richard Nixon, Gerald Ford, Jimmy Carter, George H.W. Bush and Bill Clinton were hardly *high* in likability, though they *must* have been better than average, to become presidents. (Robert Novak at one of his appearances on *The McLaughlin Group* remarked that George HW Bush was a "lousy candidate," a reason for his loss in his reelection bid, but he rationalized George W Bush's 'uninterested, disengaged, lazy style' as just fine for a president! – For Bush_43, comedian Will Ferrell joked, "working '24-7', means 24 hours a week, 7 months a year." Novak also remarked, "You don't impeach a President for lying about sex."

If I could further elaborate on the "*persecution* of Clinton," Roger Rosenblatt wrote (*Time* Magazine, Feb. 3, 1997, p. 78, before the naïve Monica Lewinsky and the villainous Kenneth Starr appeared on stage), "[Clinton] is sweet and graceful ... He works like a horse. He can weep on demand. He has spasms of inspiration. He blows up at the right people at the right times ... Yet he evokes **less warmth than much stiffer predecessors.**" (Though Donald Trump relentlessly claimed, "partisan witch hunt," in his second impeachment, seven Republican [same party] Senators voted to *convict* him. And if Sen. Mitch McConnell wanted to, he could have orchestrated a conviction of President Trump on his second impeachment, relieving the nation of so much agony, and leaving a powerful lesson for future Presidents!)

Whereas an unusually likeable and charismatic Barack Obama was awarded the Nobel Peace Prize in 2009, before he did anything, which was denied to Jimmy Carter in 1978, when both Anwar Sadat and Menachem Begin received it. Zbigniew Brzezinski, Carter's National Security Advisor, was profoundly disgusted when he learned Carter was "excluded" from the company of Sadat and Begin in 1978, as he (publicly) recalled, several years prior to his death.

As everything in behavioral science is complex and complicated, much like in economics, Obama's impact on a white majority nation with scattered racist segments embedded in it, ended up quite limited, unlike that of FDR, or Reagan. Besides, Obama's *inaction* against ISIS would be a *HUGE permanent stain*, as on Bush_43 as well, in the *post-FDR era*. Joe Biden's cruel abandonment of Afghanistan would also be a stain on his otherwise stellar presidency with surprisingly great achievements.

If I could add, what makes likeability/charisma variation in individuals? I think, we just don't know it. Until we know and have a scientific explanation, a clear grasp of it, we shall not engage in denying things that are beyond our grasp from a scientific perspective, like realizing that earth is moving around the sun, not the other way around. It maybe *fashionable* for intellectuals to deny the existence of "afterlife," or God. I would say, be humble. Accept the reality that there are innumerable things a bit like the vastness of the Cosmos beyond our grasp – There was a famous *Malayalam* [of Kerala] Poet named Kumaran Asan who wrote about this some 120 years ago, very much like this. I studied that poem in 1951, which impressed me ever since. Another was, my roommate in Medical School, Vijayaprashanthan Pillay, who became a neurosurgeon had said, unlike we sense matter, Space that occupies most of the Universe, we can't "feel" it. It stuck with me ever since – sadly, he developed Alzheimer's before his age 60.

Moderate financial inequality is thus not that consequential. But **abject poverty is,** which **must be wiped out from the face of earth.** Abject poverty has plagued humanity, over the millennia causing countless, billions of premature deaths, which could have largely been prevented with *modestly* higher progressive taxation on the affluent, and allocating the additional funds towards alleviating *hunger*, *homelessness*, and *treatable diseases,* anywhere in the world.

This can be achieved **with minimal, additional 'burden' on the affluent as taxes, far less than what we or the affluent seem to believe.**

Such a sacrifice can even be felt as *enjoyable* by the affluent when they witness **their minuscule, additional financial sacrifice has led to nearly total absence of misery in a good part of the world** - Imagine how much "joy" Bill and Melinda French Gates have had with their polio-elimination endeavor, or Jimmy Carter has had with his River Blindness Elimination Program!

Another example, among many: "Every month for more than a decade, a local farmer, Hody Childress, had made anonymous cash donations to the local pharmacy, *Geraldine Drugs*, aiming to help neighbors struggling to pay for prescription medication. The wider community learned of his good deed only after he died at age 80 in January 2023. Now, his family and donors from across the United States have vowed to continue his legacy."

Another: "Charles F. Feeney [gave away] nearly all of his $8 billion fortune to charity, much of it as quietly as he had made it, died on [Oct 9, 2023] in San Francisco.

He was 92."

MacKenzie Scott, the ex-wife of Jeff Bezos seems to be in a hurry to give away most of her fortune - by March 2024 her donations have reached $17.2 billion. She started her hefty donations months after her divorce in 2018, which she must be savoring.

Warren Buffett famously said his wealth as well as his happiness has largely been from being born in this great country (in a decent, *white*, middle class Nebraskan family, and *as male*) and the people he has been lucky enough to associate with. There are other rich folks like _George Kaiser_ subscribe to this view, of luck, or lack thereof, determining our fortunes, not entirely but to a substantial extent.

As _Richard Cohen writes in Washington Post_ in 2018 about David Letterman's interview of Barack Obama "[Eventually, they talked about luck that played in their lives]. Yes, he had talent, [Obama] said, and he had worked hard, but neither of those could fully account for how a mixed-race kid who had known his father for only one month of his childhood had wound up president of the United States. He had been lucky."

Robert H. Frank argues in his 2015 book, "*Success and Luck: Good Fortune and the Myth of Meritocracy,*" far too often, more than anything, luck plays a decisive role in our successes, including better paying jobs and building wealth. And income and wealth, as our place and country of birth, innate talents, etc., are largely a gift to us.

Thus, the wealthy are *largely* lucky, while the poor are *largely* unlucky.

Then there is also a sense, which is seldom mentioned, that the poor are *lazier,* which may have some truth to it. Industriousness is unfortunately innate to a substantial extent.

People who are born and raised in the tropics tend to be less industrious. To adapt to warm weather, they do things, especially manual labor, more slowly to prevent the body from overheating. (Marathon events are scheduled for Spring and Autumn) That slow activity creeps into mental labor as well. Most of them have no hobbies owing to *a habitual inertia* of people in the tropics. I for one have been too lazy all my life, not entirely related to my depression (see my autobiographical account at the end) and darker skin. I have been trying hard to correct it with modest but inconsistent successes.

David Landes quotes in his acclaimed 1998 book, *"The Wealth and Poverty of Nations,"* what a Bangladeshi diplomat said, "[R]ecalling his own experience and those of his compatriots when visiting temperate climes: 'In countries like India, Pakistan, Indonesia, Nigeria and Ghana I have always felt enervated by the slightest physical or *mental* exertion, whereas in the UK, France, Germany or the U.S., I have always felt reinforced and stimulated by the temperate climate, not only during long stays, but even during brief travels'."

In his diary, Albert Einstein wrote about his observations (1922-1923) for instance on **Sri Lankans who "do little, and need little.** *The simple economic cycle of life."*

Furthermore, What Robert DeNiro said about his phenomenal success as an actor is quite pertinent: In an interview on *CBS Sunday Morning* program, he said, it was his *luck* that got him there. The interviewer then remarked, he was extremely *hard working* also. DeNiro then responded, he was *lucky* enough to have the drive to work hard! The latter response may have been a mark of **humility, but not untrue**. DeNiro forced himself to gain 60Lbs for a role; he had to lose that subsequently, not a minor "*role!*"

Introduction

James Meade, a Nobel laureate in economics (1977) had said, paraphrasing, *"The frontiers of knowledge when it comes to economics keep expanding at such a rate that it is almost impossible to establish a soundly based understanding of the entire subject and its ever-evolving parts!"*

Thus, economics is an unusually complex field, but often tends to present itself as (deceptively) simple, for many to opine on aspects of it in a hurry and with (false) "confidence" - Some scholars are hesitant to label it as a branch of *science*. *Human welfare,* nonetheless, *depends on (accurately) understanding economics, towards crafting governmental policies to benefit all.*

Broadly, there are two competing "schools of thought," towards putting the principles of economics into practice: A more liberal, "left leaning" economic plan based on John Maynard Keynes's prescriptions to employ the struggling unemployed with "deficit" financing to employ them, at a living wage by "printing," so to speak, the needed currency/cash to pay them. The other, "right-leaning" one has been promoted by Friedrich August Hayek, Milton Friedman and the "*Chicago school*," which relies too much on "*free-market*" principles, without governmental interference. Scholars who subscribe to Friedman, et al, are also for low tax, as low as feasible.

There is, to me, a cruelty in advocating low tax, on those who can easily afford to pay a higher tax towards spending on programs to relieve the misery of the "least among us" and low income folks who turned out to be too "unlucky," to have a fair income but may present themselves as (deceptively) too "lazy;" even if they are genuinely lazy, you can't kill them.

Certain basic, common financial transactions such as buying things on credit and paying for them in installments by the customer based on their *estimated* (which can be tricky and risky) financial means are considered the *sine qua non,* of *economic activities*. Without that the economy will stagnate, the enormous potential of human labor for instance would remain idle.

(When I grew up in India, I have witnessed people building houses without using the credit system. [But buying everyday items, like groceries, or food in restaurants on credit (not credit cards) was quite common.] Now, they borrow, just like here most of the cost of the house. And larger and larger homes in much greater numbers are being built – The net result is that so many *more* workers are employed in the housing construction business.)

FDR (Franklin Delano Roosevelt) said in May 1932, at the depth of the Great Depression, while campaigning the first time for his presidency, ***"The country demands bold, persistent experimentation. It is common sense to take a method and try it. If it fails, admit it frankly and try another. But, above all try something."***

And FDR's last Vice President, Harry S. Truman half-jokingly asked for a "one-handed" economist to craft reliable economic policies; his economic advisers would say, 'on the one hand this would happen, if such and such a course were adopted benefitting that many, but on the other hand, that would also result in more inflation, and so on. Such prescriptions/ perceptions imply the nebulous nature of economics stressing its profound complexity.

And, we shall not be too critical of economists, owing to the great complexity of the topic, economics, as Republican Gerome Powel or Ben Bernanke have been doing. Nevertheless, we must be ready to attack economists when they pronounce economic policies with ulterior motives, such as advocating tax cuts for the well off, as Larry Kudlow or Stephen Moore, which will in all probability necessitate severe, unacceptable cuts in safety-net programs.

Two essential, *indispensable,* financial roles of governments are maintaining an adequate, but affordable national defense as well as continued funding for essential safety-net programs. Conservatives want stronger defense and more liberal spending on it while liberals want smaller defense spending and more liberal spending on safety net programs.

U.S. Federal income tax rates, History (Some rates are omitted for brevity)

History of income tax rates adjusted for inflation (1913_2013)[90][91] https://en.wikipedia.org/wiki/Income_tax_in_the_United_States						
Year	Number of brackets	First bracket	Top bracket			**Comment**
		Rate	Rate	Income	Adj. 2021 [82] [92]	
1913	7	1%	7%	$500,000	$13.7 million	First permanent income tax
1917	21	2%	67%	$2,000,000	$42.3 million	World War I financing
1918	56	6%	77%	$1,000,000	$17.2 million	—
1925	23	1.125%	25%	$100,000	$1.55 million	Post war reductions
1932	55	4%	63%	$1,000,000	$19.9 million	Depression era
1936	31	4%	79%	$5,000,000	$97.6 million	—
1941	32	10%	81%	$5,000,000	$92.1 million	World War II
1942	24	19%	88%	$200,000	$3.32 million	Revenue Act of 1942
1944	24	23%	94%	$200,000	$3.08 million	Individual Income Tax Act of 1944
1951	24	20.4%	91%	$400,000	$4.18 million	—
1954	26	20%	91%	$400,000	$4.04 million	—
1965	25	14%	70%	$200,000	$1.72 million	"JFK/LBJ" 'Tax-cut'
1971	33	14%	70%	$200,000	$1.34 million	—

1988	2	15%	28%	$29,750	$68,164	Reagan era tax cuts fully effective
1991	3	15%	31%	$82,150	$163,437	Omnibus Budget Reconciliation Act of 1990
1993	5	15%	39.6%	$89,150	$167,231	Omnibus Budget Reconciliation Act of 1993
2003	6	10%	35%	$311,950	$451,531	Bush tax cuts
2013	7	10%	39.6%	$400,000	$465,314	American Taxpayer Relief Act of 2012
2018	7	10%	37%	$500,000	$510 thousand	Tax Cuts and Jobs Act of 2017

We may have to accept/tolerate a *modicum* of "waste" in financing these twin financial necessities. As an example, in the U.S., compared with *almost* all other developed countries, the waste that has crept up in healthcare spending is far too large. Too large amounts the government pays for certain defense department procurements are well known. Since such expenditures are well-known, it is also necessary to keep a good eye on such "wastes" and try to bring them down as much as feasible.

And FDR, through deficit spending of the New Deal provided substantial relief, as he labeled to the *"Army of Unemployed."* However, the Roosevelt administration wasn't too sure about the rationale for "unrestrained," continuation of deficit financing of various New Deal programs.

By 1936, they applied the brake on the New Deal deficit spending endeavors, towards balancing the budget. That indeed led to a recession on the recovering Great Depression. The unemployment rate spiked from about 14% in 1937 to 17% in 1939. But soon WWII (World War II) broke out when greatly enhanced deficit financing along with very high taxation on the affluent, up to 94% on over about $3 million (in 2020 dollars), wiping out the Depression.

This led many to argue that the *New Deal* didn't cure the Great Depression, WWII did.

But a war employing huge numbers of people to produce war materiel, which are destined to be largely destroyed eventually creates essentially "non-productive" labor/employment, compared with employing comparable number of people to build, say a *Hoover Dam or a Grand Coulee Dam* supplying water and electricity to millions for essential needs, including irrigation to enhance agricultural output, or building roads, railways including underground and high-speed rail system, creates productive, beneficial jobs.

A Historical Note on U.S. Income Tax

Regular, federal individual income tax, which was designed as a progressive levy on Americans' incomes became effective in 1913. The progressive rates have fluctuated greatly reflecting the then need, etc., including the philosophy on social and defense spending by the then administration in power, along with the make-up of the Congress.

A seldom mentioned fact is that our grasp of how taxes in general are designed and collected is woefully inadequate. Bruce Bartlett, an aficionado on taxation, who wrote extensively on the topic and was a senior adviser to Presidents Ronald Reagan and George H.W. Bush wrote, "Congress had no idea how many tax loopholes there were or how much revenue they were costing the Treasury."

As an illustration of the complexity, the top state income tax rate *in Missouri is only 5.4%, on ALL (taxable) incomes over $8,600, for single or joint filers, while in California it is 13.3%, on taxable incomes over $1 million,* but paradoxically most Californians pay at an appreciably lower rate in state income tax than most Missourians do. -- *Up to $17,864, state income tax in California, for joint filers* *is only 2%; 4% applies only on over $42,350; and 6% applies only on over $66,842.*

Between 1942 and 1981, in the "FDR era" (1933-1980) the top (marginal) federal income tax rates of between 70% and 94% were on over between about $613,000 and $3 million, in 2020 dollars.

In a capitalist country like the U.S. those rates probably **were too high on over such LOW amounts**. Before 1942, however, similar top rates were on over about $17-to-$93 million in 2020 dollars, which were quite reasonable, I believe. Therefore, **rather than the rates, what matters is the amount over which each rate is set**.

It is worth noting that in the 1936 tax reform, there were 31 different rates from 4% to 79%, the top rate of 79% was on over $5 million ($93 million in 2020 dollars) but was meant to be collected from just *one taxpayer*, John D. Rockefeller. If you analyze the various rates of 1936 tax reform plan, a majority of households paid only 4% on their incomes, as the **8% federal income tax started at Taxable incomes over $74,477** in 2020 dollars; **below that, after deductions, the federal income tax rate was only 4%**; 10% tax rate applied only on over $148,955! (I checked my figures repeatedly, still I have doubts, as the figures don't *look* right. I would ask the readers to check my figures.)

Whereas, with the 1986 tax reform, **the top rate of just 28% was on over $29,750 ($65,100 in 2020 dollars),** which *millions* had to pay. **These two tax laws must have had vastly different impacts on the taxpayers.**

And now, if the top income households in the U.S. were to have a substantially higher marginal rate of say, **70% but only on over say, $50 million** (not $1 million, as before 1981) **of their taxable incomes, the additional revenue could run in hundreds of billions**, but without squeezing lower-income taxpayers – *The mega rich would still only pay at the lower rates as everyone else on their incomes below that* (very high) *critical level*, which may not be clear to many, if not most.

Average Tax Rates for the Highest-Income Taxpayers, 1945-2009

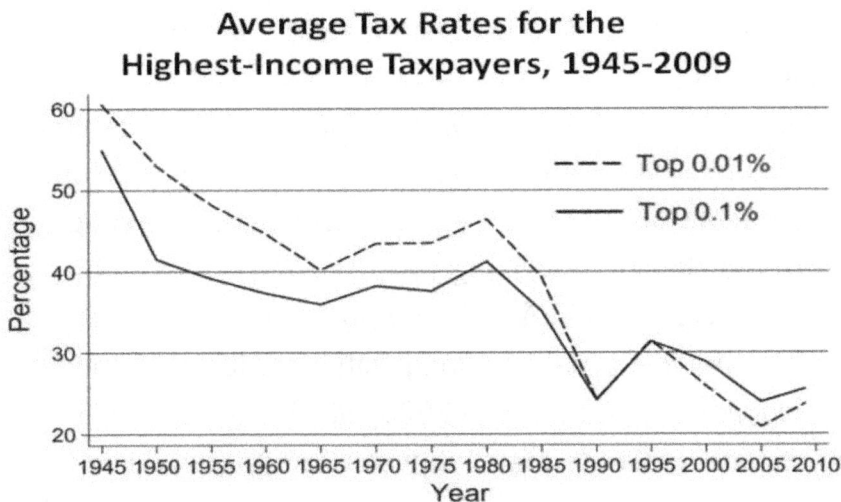

Source: CRS calculations using Internal Revenue Service (IRS) Statistics of Income (SOI) information.

(Fig. 1): <https://upload.wikimedia.org/wikipedia/commons/e/e8/US_high-income_effective_tax_rates.png>

This figure 1 is unusually important in that it may illustrate why the financial inequality went up back to the Depression era level, as Robert Reich shows in the suspension bridge-like nature of inequality, largely, may not entirely be, a Reaganomics effect!

The Reagan tax-cuts caused a steadily rising financial inequality, along with hunger and homelessness for far too many poor Americans. Even the modest Bush_41 tax hike of 1991, or a further significant Clinton tax-hikes had only modest benefits to the poor. The 1996 Welfare reform added to the misery of the poor. Then the rather drastic (Bush_43) tax-cuts of 2001 and 2003 further aggravated the burgeoning inequality:

See "*The Price of Inequality*," By Joseph Stiglitz, 2012. Watch Stiglitz on <u>*<booktv.org>*</u> for a quick *exposé* of this book.

In the 1986 tax-reform act, which was also touted even by some liberal Democratic law makers, like Sen. Bill Bradley (D-NJ), there were just *two rates* only, a top rate of 28% as said above. And a substantial 15% on any taxable income below that. *The total income tax revenue to the treasury fell only modestly/moderately from when the top rate was over 90%, but the bulk of the income tax revenue was from the broad middle class* (lower, middle, and upper middle classes) *excusing the rich from shouldering their prior responsibility of paying the bulk of the federal income tax.* This situation, along with other factors like too low minimum wage ($7.25 in 2023, which ought to be [inflation adjusted] >$14 to match that of 1968[!]), (but ought to be more like >$20/hour when the rise in productivity along with rise in per capita, inflation adjusted income. Indeed, that's exactly what Gov. Gavin Newsome did in <u>California, raising the minimum wage of Fast-Food workers to $20/hour from April 2024</u>) imperceptibly led to a steadily rising (income and wealth) inequality, as we experience now.

That unfair tax reform plan was slightly corrected by George HW Bush, who raised the top rate to 31%. Bill Clinton raised the top rate further to a much more reasonable rate of 39.6%. However, the first (lowest) tax rate was still the too high 15%, which ought to be 5%, if not lower. But Income tax revenue rose appreciably with both tax hikes. Clinton was able to balance the budget, which was unnecessary, even dangerous, especially because George W. Bush used the modest surplus, as an excuse, so to speak to have tax-cuts, which were **deep when he cut the capital gains tax in 2003 to 15% with having the** *carried interest loophole, which for many ran up to billions a year in income -* John Paulson's haul for 2007 and 2010 together was *$7.9 billion,* not million*. His federal income tax was probably all of 15% on that $7.9 billion, not that much higher than what many poor people pay as sales taxes, up to 12%!* (Dennis Kozlowski, of Tyco International, in 2006 had agreed "to pay $21.2 million to settle charges of avoiding New York sales tax on 12 paintings....")

The modest reduction in revenue from the Reagan-tax-cuts put a steadily rising pressure on social spending with an endless call to reduce "unnecessary" spending on safety-net programs – Remember the welfare queen?

When genuine, conscientious Republicans with high work ethic, promote the idea of "conservative's small government," they mean cuts in social/safety-net spending, to encourage, even coerce, people, many of whom don't work very hard, to develop a better work ethic. Their recommendations to cut the spending "with starve the beast mentality," however, are too cruel, but they don't sense the cruelty behind their proposals. They *ignore the too low minimum wage* and other factors that make the *income of the poor too low;* they tend to assume that people are generally paid according to *"what they are worth." Some of them may see the cruelty behind their proposals but they just don't care.*

Share of Federal Tax Revenue

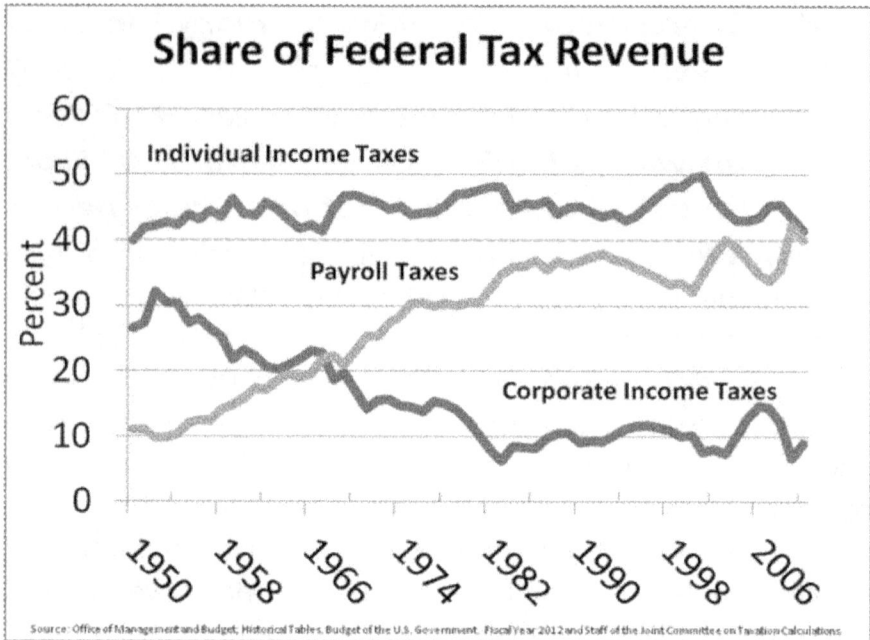

Figure 2.

Binyamin Appelbaum and Robert Gebeloff write, "According to an analysis by *The New York Times* [2012], Congress cut federal taxation at every income level over the last 30 years. ***State and local taxes, meanwhile, increased for most*** [*especially, lower income*] ***Americans.*** ... ***Households earning more than $200,000 benefited from the largest percentage declines in total taxation as a share of income.*** ... The average American in 2010 paid 30% more of income in payroll taxes than in 1980, even while paying 27% less in federal income taxes. As a result, revenue from the payroll tax almost equaled income tax revenue [see figure 2]. [Meanwhile] income inequality rose to the highest level since the Great Depression."

(The above 2012 New York Times piece is the most relevant article that supports my arguments.)

Appelbaum appears to be quite enraged to bluntly state in a 2021 piece, "Resistance to taxation is the rotten core of the modern Republican Party!"

Modest as well as Vastly Discordant Remunerations: Examples

Modest Discordance: The knowledge, skill/dexterity and effort required for a cook at a McDonald's (in California, until April 2024) and those of a United Autoworkers' Union worker are fairly comparable but the autoworker with pension and other benefits makes <u>nearly four times more</u>, as well as job security. Caitlin Clark's new salary for 2024 is only $76,535, while the number one NBA draft pick Victor Wembanyama "will be paid a whopping $12 million for his first year in the league." And yet, she, who maybe a rare exception, single-handedly attracted the maximum number of nearly <u>19 million viewers</u>, ahead of any basketball game, men's or women's in the last four seasons! However, she landed a Nike endorsement deal, <u>worth $28 million</u>. This $28 million pay, over eight years is not entirely luck, one could infer.

There are numerous such examples where the workers' qualifications/skill and effort seldom correlate with the remunerations they get. And it is not an illogical argument that ***few are paid corresponding to what they and their jobs are actually worth; your "luck,"*** largely determines whether you're at a "well-paying" job or not. And (modestly) *progressive taxation is thus justified,* even a necessity as well as *a logical remedy.*

Extreme discordance: The top 25 hedge fund managers together raked in close to $100 billion for the five years from 2009-to-2013, *for their (socially) unimportant job*, and then paying close to 15% (23.8%, from 2013) in federal income tax!

John Paulson's haul for 2007 and 2010 together, as said above, was *$7.9 billion*. And Steven A. Cohen of former SAC Capital raked in *$2.3 billion* in 2013. Eight of Cohen's traders were either convicted or pleaded guilty for insider trading charges. Mathew Martoma, a senior trader at SAC with a colorful past, finished his sentence in July 2021. *Cohen himself had to pay $1.8 billion as criminal* and civil *penalty that year, still pocketing a cool $500 million,* and no jail-time! (Imagine, *if these humungous earners were taxed at 70% on over $50 million, not over $1 million* as they used to pay in the pre-Reagan era, on their earnings that may cover a good portion of the mortgage payments of the default home-loans of low-income ("NIJA" – No Income, Job or assets) homeowners who lost their homes during the 2007-2009 housing crisis and/or the installment payments of a good chunk of the student loan debt.

John Paulson's billions was probably largely from *cleverly* [in addition to being clever, one has to be quite lucky too] predicting that housing crisis and "shorting" subprime mortgage-backed securities. Further, Goldman Sachs also made billions essentially by betting against (shorting) the subprime mortgage-backed securities, as Paulson did, which Goldman had already recommended to many of their "regular" customers to buy!

Whereas, Capt. Sully Sullenberger who probably saved the lives of all 155 on board by skillfully landing the crippled *USAir flight 1547 on the Hudson river* on January 14, 2009, was paid in the neighborhood of $135,000, annually, which may be better than the median wage, but pittance when the value of his job is factored in - On December 28, 2014, pilot error was attributed to the loss of 162 lives when an identical plane lost control and fell into South China Sea. Sullenberger's skill with amazing 'presence of mind' probably can be seen only in 0.1% or in less of us, as in say, super athletes, like Caitlin Collins, LeBron James and Michael Jordan. But most of those super athletes make so much money, in addition to receiving public adoration. There are many unsung-hero soldiers who may have Sullenberger's skills, or close to it, and may have saved numerous lives, as did the *Seal Team* 6 that took out bin Laden in 2011. (**Compare Sullenberger's response to that of Pedro Arredondo,** the Uvalde [TX] School District Police Chief as well as of Scot Peterson, the security officer at Parkland.)

Alarmingly, Commuter Airline pilots used to be paid even less than $30,000 annually. Many of them couldn't afford to rent a comfortable motel room, and might sleep in their cars, or bunk with others to save money. In the commuter plane crash of Colgan Air flight 3407 on February 12, 2009, on its way from Newark, NJ to Buffalo, NY that killed all 49 on board, a year-long investigation "found the probable cause to be the pilots' inappropriate response to the 'stall' warnings," (due to fatigue from lack of sleep?) But criticisms abound about airline companies, for charging "high fees" for baggage and for every little added convenience, which used to be free, but when the ticket prices were far higher prior to 1980s, nearly ten times higher! However, following the Colgan Air crash, their salary has substantially improved to have an average salary of $86,579 annually, as of July 2023.

After years of losing money and repeated bankruptcies, airline companies have been finally becoming profitable (until the coronavirus pandemic) but with such *drastic* and *dangerous* cost-cutting measures.

It appears the Airline companies had (figuratively) signed a "suicide pact," to declare bankruptcies over and over again, while the Drug companies have formed a most powerful "cartel," to raise drug-prices, making them *far* beyond the reach of *most* who need those (lifesaving) drugs. **These two contrasting business models have been operating in the same free-market system!**

 Such inconsistencies are an illustration of the built-in flaw that creeps up not infrequently into *the* free-market system.

Nevertheless, Pfizer deserves commendation for letting poorer countries to manufacture a generic version of their recently patented (Nov. 2021) Covid-19 drug!

(Millions of AIDS victims perished in Sub-Saharan Africa, prior to the advent of the magic, three-drug-cocktail in 1996 [the discoverer, David Ho incidentally has largely been unappreciated, other than by *TIME* Magazine. I thought he would get a Nobel Prize in Medicine around the year 2000. Did his **non-Japanese** East Asian ethnicity play a role? *His* **Wikipedia** site says **David Da-i Ho ...** is a Taiwanese American AIDS researcher, physician, and virologist who has made a number of scientific contributions to the understanding and treatment of HIV infection. .... He championed for combination anti-retroviral therapy instead of single therapy, **which turned** HIV **from absolute** *terminal disease* **into a** *chronic disease*. [Whereas, "Austrian physician Julius Wagner-Jauregg in 1917 used fever therapy, which was only partially effective, for the treatment of neurosyphilis for which he received the 1927 Nobel Prize in Physiology or Medicine] The cost per patient-year was over $10,000, generic versions of which, since 2003 or so, have been procured for around $150!)

An estimated 25 million lives have been saved with the Antiretroviral treatment, far more in Sub-Saharan Africa than elsewhere, *most of whom as a result of the discovery of the "three-drug cocktail,"* (procured for around $150, instead of $10,000, which Africans could not afford to buy) along with preventing millions of kids from becoming AIDS orphans!

And though George W Bush wrecked Iraq and Syria so badly, he allocated $15 billion for AIDS treatment, etc., in 2003, which was praised by then Senate majority leader Bill Frist (R-TN, and a surgeon); that may have saved millions of lives in Sub-Saharan Africa. Black Africans 'worship' Bush_43, for saving so many of their loved ones' lives. But Bill Clinton had a still more critical role in eliminating the patent protection of that AIDS cocktail for low-income countries in 2000.

Perhaps, not practical but *I would propose for the U.S. Treasury to pay the entire R&D* (Research and Development) *budget of all U.S. based drug companies, in exchange for giving up the patent protection of the FDA* (Federal Drug administration) *approved drugs*. In return, when a drug is approved by the FDA, the maker ought to get a handsome prizemoney, based on the approximate (lifesaving) value of each drug. The companies then can conduct extensive research on orphan drugs and on discovering/inventing novel antibiotics without worrying about the cost of such research. About half of the prizemoney ought to be shared by the research team as an incentive for them toil hard while the other half goes to the company under whose auspices the research was conducted.

The financial aspect of pharmaceutical research, the total R&D budget of all the U.S. based pharmaceutical companies together is in the neighborhood of $100 billion, per year. The annual cost to U.S. customers is about $370 billion for the drugs they purchase. A rough estimate of the annual cost of drugs to the U.S. taxpayers/customers then would be around $150 billion, as drug companies would receive R&D reimbursement, plus say $50 billion as prizemoney. (Much of that $370 billion is shouldered by insurance companies. But the Insurance companies have to recoup their expenses with higher premiums.) The U.S. taxpayers would still save around $70 billion annually in drug prices. If the U.S. eliminates the patent-protection, there is a fair chance for the rest of the world to follow. More than that, the prohibitive high prices of certain drugs prevent many less well-off consumers not to avail themselves of their benefits.

Furthermore, the unique benefit of this endeavor is that it will be the most cost-effective foreign aid the developed countries can bestow on developing countries.

The Rationale for Progressive Taxation

As described above, *discordance in the distribution of income and wealth is largely a function of luck. And in a civilized harmonious society, the "lucky" are expected to lend a handsome, but reasonable helping hand to the unlucky.* In wars soldiers would go to extremes often risking their own lives not to leave wounded comrades behind. (Even in the animal kingdom, for example members of an elephant herd, usually led by a matriarch, make sure the weaker are not left behind.)

And *progressive taxation is a fair way to mitigate far too wider distributional discordance of income and wealth*, which has been worsening during most of the past several decades, since the beginning of the Reagan era, both at home and abroad. By taxing the "luckier," at *moderately* higher rates, *modest, but far less than equal, redistribution* of the benefits of incomes, could be provided to the less "lucky." Unfortunately, *there is a pervasive notion that paying higher taxes by the affluent is "unjust."* Paying a *modestly* higher amount in taxes, by the affluent is beneficial to *most*, including many of the affluent. And only a "tiny" segment among the highest income group, who are immensely rich and can easily afford need to shell out much of that higher tax. (The "giving pledge" initiated by billionaires Bill Gates and Warren Buffett in 2010 was a reaction to the huge, burgeoning inequality both at home and abroad. A catalyst for this endeavor/ mentality may have been Ted Turner who publicly announced in 1997 that he would be donating $1 billion to the United Nations, which was about half or more of his then newly created net worth, out of his good luck!)

Further, if they appreciate, as they ought to, their (modestly) bigger taxes have relieved the misery of huge numbers of people, *humans,* very much like them, including many abroad. As said elsewhere, the ***extra amount they need to pay is a lot less than what they think they needed to pay*** if the rates were not higher.

Nevertheless, with so much progress humanity has made so far, as Nicholas Kristof writes, "2017 was probably the very best year in the long history of humanity," despite as bad as things have been with so much misery around. But it could have been far better with ***minimal additional burden on the well-off***, and long before 2017.

According to a (Henry) Kaiser Family Foundation study, "The large body of research on the effects of Medicaid expansion under the ACA (Affordable Care Act) suggests it has had largely positive impacts on coverage; access to care, [affordability], including impacts on state budgets, uncompensated care costs for hospitals and clinics, ..." And if the ACA, a.k.a. 'Obamacare' were repealed, as repeatedly attempted by the Republican Congress as well as the Trump administration, it "would result in 217,000 additional deaths over the next decade." (Those *attempts* already have had a negative impact. As Sarah Kliff writes in *Vox*, the percentage of uninsured has risen from 10.9% in November 2016 to 12.2% in December 2017, according to Gallup.

However, though the results are still not fully clear or known, ACA has been a substantial plus. *Before ACA, there weren't many standards for what a health insurance company could and could not cover. One in four Americans have a preexisting health condition! Health insurance now generally covers more procedures, including mental health and maternity care. And millions more low income-Americans now have quality and affordable health insurance.*

On Tax-hikes on The Rich

Many superrich like Warren Buffett, Bill Gates and George Kaiser are for raising taxes on the rich like them. Gates also advocates taxing investment income (the bulk of his income) at the <u>same rate</u> as wage income; <u>in 2014, he had</u> <u>proposed a 'progressive tax on consumption, on buying yachts and private jets'</u>. *In addition to investment income, any income one gets, say from borrowing from one's wealth also ought to be taxed as regular, wage income.*

Warren Buffett wrote, *"While the poor and <u>middle class</u> fight for us in Afghanistan, and while most Americans struggle to make ends meet, we the mega rich continue to get our extraordinary tax breaks,"* NY Times, Aug 14, 2011.

The 2003 drastic, capital gains-tax cut to 15% on up to multibillion-dollar incomes (including investment and hedge-fund-managing commission incomes, applying "carried interest" loophole) *enormously widened the financial inequality by reducing taxes on top 0.01% incomes to <u>22% by 2005, which was near 60% at around 1945</u>* (Fig.1)!

Average Tax Rates for the Highest-Income Taxpayers, 1945-2009

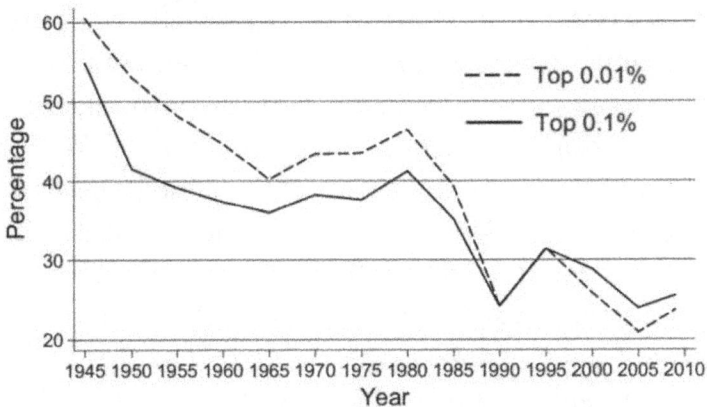

Source: CRS calculations using Internal Revenue Service (IRS) Statistics of Income (SOI) information.

In November *2017 over 400 millionaires and billionaires wrote to Congress asking not to cut their taxes*, instead raise them; the patriotic millionaires have been doing so since 2010. But such pleas were to no avail.

And former New York City Mayor Michael Bloomberg strongly attacked the 2017 tax law, calling it "an economically indefensible blunder that will harm our future." However, he didn't support raising taxes on the rich. He says if the taxes are raised, the rich who can afford to move away would do so. This *"Bloomberg attitude,"* as against the attitudes of *comparably conscientious* Warren Buffett or Bill & Melinda French Gates, or George Kaiser or umpteen other immensely rich *who WANT to pay higher taxes*, is a telling example of why we have so much inequality and misery in the world. *The rich aren't that much less conscientious than the rest of us*, *but they fail to see as Michael Bloomberg doesn't, their reluctance to pay higher taxes, which wouldn't make them significantly any LESS RICH is the principal cause of misery the poor endure*.

In a 2017 *New York Times* piece, Steven Rattner writes, ***"I have been a substantial beneficiary of the so-called 'carried interest' loophole***, the tax provision that provides an indefensibly lower tax rate on profits earned by ... hedge fund operators, real estate developers (presumably including President Trump) and the like."

Furthermore, International Monetary Fund (IMF) finds that raising taxes on the rich to reduce inequality would not hurt growth. Even Steve Bannon, Donald Trump's former 'chief strategist' actually wanted to raise taxes on the rich, unlike his other advisors, like Larry Kudlow or Stephen Moore.

Unfortunately, with the 2017 "Tax Cuts and Jobs Act," the Republican Congress cut the taxes of the rich when the financial (income and wealth) inequality has been so high and kept on rising. Furthermore, the 2017 Tax cuts bill despite "that the economy grew in 2018, and in the absence of another policy that could have caused a large revenue loss, the *data imply that the 2017 tax cut substantially reduced revenues*."

Oxfam (January 22, 2018) reports, "Richest 1% bagged 82% of [global] wealth created [in 2017 while the] poorest half of humanity got nothing." United States is no exception, as the richest three men (*two of them, however, wanted their taxes substantially raised*) have more wealth than the bottom half of all U.S. households, as described below. Nick Hanauer and David Rolf write in *TIME* magazine, *"The Top 1% of Americans Have Taken $50 Trillion From the Bottom 90%—And That's Made the U.S. Less Secure."*

Although moderate tax-cuts on corporate profits have been widely recommended, the 2017 cuts have been too drastic and would again mostly help the affluent. The carried interest loophole continued, though Donald Trump railed against it during the 2016 election season.

Taxes in the U.S. have been far less progressive since the beginning of the Reagan era, through Bush_43's

2003 capital gain tax-cuts, with some respite during the Clinton administration and since 2013, until the Trump tax cuts of 2017.

Andrew Ross Sorkin writes, "[The 2017 'Tax Cuts and Jobs Act'] benefit[s] the 'ultra-rich' ... A real estate investor, Jason Harbor, who will probably be a beneficiary of the tax plan, wrote on Twitter: 'Why are my taxes going down and my assistant's is going up? Can someone explain how that is fair'?"

It ought to be made clear, as a rule, almost all tax-cuts benefit the affluent and hurt the poor and low-income folks, while almost all tax-hikes benefit the poor and low-income folks, while depleting the affluent's incomes.

The *Economist reports,* "Americans appear to be less averse to inequality than citizens of other rich countries. ... *actual CEO-to-unskilled wage ratio in America is 354-to-1 [about ten times more than what Americans think]*. ... In 2014, taxes and transfers reduced American inequality by a mere 18%; this compares with 25% in Britain, 29% in Germany and 34% in France." If "taxes and transfers" were to rise as in, say France or Germany, with significantly higher progressive taxation as this piece advocates, the rising inequality could be sufficiently checked, even reversed, which is what is needed.

In the 2016 election season, all seventeen Republican presidential candidates dutifully displayed their drastic tax-cut proposals, which *obligatorily* benefit the rich.

(None of those seventeen probably had an *accurate grasp* of how cruel their proposals were, as Bruce Bartlett or some of those candidates' economic advisors had, which may even *absolve them of the cruelty embedded in their proposals*.)

There appears to be a blind spot and/or ignorance in the *Republican leaders'* vision in that, more than anything, their *identity is inextricably dependent on income tax-cuts,* almost exclusively benefiting the affluent, which is **about the opposite of how President Eisenhower felt**.

Some of the advocates for the rich cleverly couch the wording of tax-cuts on the pretext that tax-cuts for the rich, a.k.a. "job-creators" would help the nation's economy in the long run, eventually benefitting all, the erstwhile **'trickle-down-economics'**.

The principal reason why it is a lot easier to cut taxes for the rich than to raise on them, who can easily afford to pay higher taxes, **the potential beneficiaries of higher taxes on the rich, the poor, and low-income folks do not sense the "pain" of tax-cuts for the rich, unlike when they need to pay higher prices for say, groceries**. And Republicans managed to cut taxes when they gained power, about again and again!

As an ideal goal, I would suggest, for a given country or a governmental entity, **the upper limit of pay/income may be under 100-fold higher than the lowest pay/income**, and the **wealth-disparity** may not exceed **1,000-fold.** When those limits are breached, say for three consecutive years, they ought to be rectified with **a built-in formula for higher taxation of the affluent**.

Our Poor Grasp of Taxation in General

We all pay taxes. And are acutely aware of it too. But we (wrongly) assume if (the progressive) federal income tax is raised it would be a greater burden on the middle class, as it is on the rich; the latter have been paying less and less federal income taxes since 1980s. *If the (progressive) federal income tax is raised, the bottom 70%, if not 95%, would pay hardly more while they, imperceptibly perhaps, benefit in different ways such as from increased spending to improve public services as well as spending more on safety-net programs.* It would ordinarily affect the top 5-to-30% based on how the higher taxation is set on various income groups. Whereas, if the local taxes, especially sales taxes, are raised, the lowest income groups would be hurt most. *The bottom fifth in incomes pays seven times more in sales taxes as a share of their income than the "top 1%" does.* Sales taxes are quite regressive but easy to raise specifically for one or another necessary local need usually by a quarter-cent at a time often with local ballot measures.

And as *ProPublica uncovered, some of the richest pay minuscule amounts in federal income tax!* They borrow handsome amounts against their wealth to maintain their luxurious lifestyle and other needs, which would then keep their taxable incomes to be low and they don't need to pay much as income tax. As suggested above, such incomes ought to be treated as regular income, to be taxed as such. Wall Street Journal reports Elon Musk *borrowed $1 Billion from SpaceX* around the time he acquired *Twitter*. If that $1 billion were his regular, taxable income, he would have to pay about >$500 million (or >$750 million if it were before 1980) more in federal and state income taxes!

Warren Buffett repeated in 2013, "he's still paying at a lower tax rate than his secretary," as his income was reported mostly as "capital gain" despite a higher tax bill in 2013 than in 2012. Many conservative pundits and their minions unabashedly repeated their *mantra*, "If Buffett thinks he's not paying enough tax, why not him write a check to the IRS and send it?"

A telling example is what happened in 2010 in Washington state. "The plan devised by [Bill Gates Sr.] to slap a 5% tax on earnings over $200,000 -- Initiative Measure 1098 -- was rejected by 65% of voters," despite that more than 90% of those who voted against it wouldn't be paying any state income tax with that ballot measure if it had passed. Even if at a later date, some of their incomes go over $200K, they will have to pay a bit but insignificant amount more.

Steve Balmer and others cruelly campaigned against this initiative started by the father of Balmer's boss, Bill Gates [Jr.] somehow succeeded.

Most low-income households, around 45% of the total, pay no federal (individual) income tax, **but they do pay,** along with the middle class, disproportionately *FAR*

MORE IN FEDERAL PAYROLL TAX as a share of their incomes compared with the affluent, which was left untouched in the 2017 tax-law**.**

It should be stressed a ***widespread, deep-rooted belief prominently*** exists that ***the 'poor and low income'*** *folks pay NO federal (income) tax while they gain SO MUCH from the government, from us, the taxpayers! This concept is a cruel travesty* cleverly and effectively *perpetrated by* (some of) *the affluent.* This is not to disregard that many poor would look for freebees rather than "struggle" by working for it, which may not be that rare either. Again, *such unseemly scenes exist almost entirely because the MINIMUM WAGE is ridiculously LOW.*

Ideally, *all states ought to have ballots in place similar to what California did in 2012 to raise revenue from higher income folks* so that local taxes could be cut to help out poor folks. *Progressive Democrats in all states ought to galvanize to put these measures on the ballots, whenever feasible* – If I could add, back in 2016, I believe, when a reporter asked Hillary Clinton about "cutting" payroll tax, she was uninterested, saying, paraphrasing, "When the payroll tax-cut ended, nobody said anything about it." It may also be because there are few who would advocate for cutting regressive taxes as the constant, vocal plea for cutting progressive taxes, cleverly put out by too many of the affluent, which helps them, whereas the former helps the poor and the middle class.

Nevertheless, it's true, low income-groups are helped by social safety-net programs such as SNAP (Supplemental Nutritional Assistance Program - Food Stamps), Earned Income Tax Credit (EITC), Medicaid, disability benefits and temporary welfare, which are far too restricted in the U.S. compared with other affluent countries making the life of the lowest income groups quite tough; *many of them experience hunger and eviction as a constant threat adding to their misery*.

Those among the lower income groups who pay federal income taxes and some in the middle class would get some tax-cuts with the 2017 tax-cut law but comparatively far smaller than what the rich get as tax-cuts. The doubling of standard deduction in it benefits those who pay federal income tax but do not "itemize."

Many among the poor, especially in inner-city areas, are subjected to constant threat of <u>violence and senseless murders</u> (Listen to an unusually touching <u>interview of Jill Leovy</u> on '*NPR-Fresh-Air*' on January 26, 2015 on her book, ***Ghettoside. This interview is so gripping with a unique inflection in the tone of Leovy's voice, with profound empathy*** she, as a white woman displays with the mothers of black murder victims, who have been mostly ignored by the society, ***especially when the perpetrators are also black***, including by the black middle class? It's convenient to be indifferent to this predicament as both perpetrators and victims are [mostly black (male) youths])

(Wikipedia: "Jill Leovy is an American journalist and nonfiction writer. She is best known for her 2015 *New York Times* best-seller book, '*Ghettoside: A True Story of Murder in America*', about homicide in <u>Los Angeles</u>. **Leovy argues** in *Ghettoside* that *more effort must be given to arresting and incarcerating perpetrators of <u>inner-city murders,</u> because 'impunity for the murder of black men* [by other black men, but not by Police or Whites] remained America's great, though mostly invisible, race problem'.")*Ghettoside* opens with an unusually touching real life-story of a younger black mother irresistibly sniffing a pair of sneakers her murdered 15-or-16-year-old son wore, when received from a white police officer.

<u>On April 27, 2015, a Baltimore mom</u>, a single, physically fit mother of six, in her thirties, repeatedly hit her taller and stronger 16-year-old son, without thinking about the cameras around; the teenager did not resist, other than running away to protect his head, and passively took the beatings, when

he couldn't be away from her. Unlike the prevailing notion of younger black men being constantly harassed and victimized by the Police, here the mom was apparently blaming her son for participating in a riot, for the heck of it, as she saw a rock in his hand. She said, "That's my only son, and at the end of the day, I don't want him to be a Freddie Gray." Later she said, when she caught him, he said, "okay, mom, okay mom, ..." before trying to run away from her to avoid the beatings, by recognizing his deviation from the way she raised him!

Historical Attempts to Reduce Incorrigible Inequality

Our innate altruism, which has been sharpened by religious, or idealistic belief systems, prompted us to strive for substantially lessening, if not eliminating misery in people around us, but with very, very limited overall success.

Jesus Christ, when viewed as human, and numerous conscientious Christians, the like of Pope Francis and St. (Mother) Teresa as well as Karl Marx, Mahatma Gandhi, Jawaharlal Nehru, Fidel Castro, Salvador Allende, Aneurin Bevan and quite a few Democratic leaders like Bernie Sanders, George McGovern, Bill Clinton, and Alexandria Ocasio-Cortez strongly advocated socialism or socialist policies. But Marx, unlike Christ, specifically advocated violence (a fatal flaw of Marxism/Communism) to abate *atrocious*, financial inequality but without any real "global" success.

Indeed, the twentieth century had witnessed ***enormous misery and millions of deaths from brutal violence and extensive, unnecessary starvation, emanated in the process of implementing Marxism, in the Soviet Union, China, North Korea and Cambodia!*** This horrific misery unleashed on the masses may have been an inherent defect of Marxism (However, Marxist revolutions, as the French revolution, are an inevitable consequence of persisting, profound inequality!)

Then again, the conditions under which Marxism was adopted, or by **the nature of the LEADERS who "used" Marxism, say as Josef Stalin did, as against Nikita Khrushchev, or Mikhail Gorbachev reacted** to Stalin's horrific Brutality, could have been a *decisive factor* for the incalculable misery the people had to endure under Stalin, who may have gratuitously <u>starved nearly four million Ukrainians to death</u> by confiscating their food grains between 1931 and 1934! And unlike the Kims of N. Korea, or the Khmer Rouge whose brutality could be compared with the Holocaust, **Ho Chi Minh was a benevolent but determined leader**. Furthermore, the **Vietnamese quelled one of the most brutal treatments of the populace in history by the Khmer Rouge in Cambodia** (Ho Chi Minh died in 1969, however.) – Even <u>George McGovern</u> <u>advocated U.S. military intervention in Cambodia</u> in 1978! Sen. Jack Danforth (R-MO) with two other Democratic Senators initiated famine relief there in 1979.

In the Southern Indian state of Kerala, following the clear, electoral victory of the Communist party in 1957, there was **a very small chance** for EMS Namboodiripad, as conscientious as he had been, to unleash brutal violence, the effect of Marxist ideology [!] if he had unlimited control without the *supervision* of the Central Government, which dismissed the EMS government, probably prematurely, after two years! (EMS donated his immense wealth to the Communist party; towards the end of his life, he lived comfortably with the "charity" of the party. When he died at 88, the then Chief Minister of Kerala, of his party, couldn't control his sorrow and burst into tears.)

There have also been substantial successes with Marxism at a small scale in certain parts of the world, but few readers would agree with me if I wrote about the **success of Marxism under Fidel Castro** about 100 miles from the Florida coast. Cuba achieved phenomenal success in providing a fairly good quality of life to *all* its citizens – free universal, quality healthcare has been provided to have a lower infant mortality than in the USA!

As an Indian American, it is painful for me to see the persistent poverty in India, especially in the rural Northern India.

Some ten million bonded laborers live and work, along with their children, in virtual slavery in India still! Tens of millions of untouchables remain untouchable in India. Compared with casteism in many parts of India, the racism anywhere in the **post-slavery** USA is and has been much less malignant, I believe. A sizable minority of the *Dalits* (Untouchables) in India do not look much different from many Indian Brahmins. Kamala Harris's mother, Shyamala Gopalan Harris was a Tamil Brahmin. She raised her daughters, Kamala and Maya, as "black girls." Tamil Brahmins are looked upon as highly gifted intellectuals and artists, by other Indians. The two Indian born Nobel Prize winners in Physics and the only one in Chemistry and the famous Mathematician Srinivasa Ramanujan who died at 32 have been Tamil Brahmins, so are Sundar Pichai, Indira Nui and Raghuram Rajan who correctly predicted 2007-08 Great Recession, in 2005 for which he was mocked by some senior economists, then.

India has some 140 billionaires, worth over $800 billion, which they accumulated mostly by exploiting poorer/less well-off Indians – Mukesh Ambani is worth over $100 billion, lives in the most expensive residence in the world with four helipads, costing close to $2 billion to build, but next to *Dharavi*, where the slum-residents had only one toilet per 1,440 residents [!] in 2006, but in February 2022, "the largest public toilet in the country" was opened in Dharavi.

Should so much disparity be allowed to exist in a democracy?

If India's rich were taxed, and collected at a reasonable rate, that would generate enough funds for satisfactory sanitation, safe drinking water, and basic housing for *almost* all Indians. That was already achieved in the Southern Indian State of Kerala by about 1995, which indeed was largely, not entirely, an achievement of the Communist party there (along with a successful family planning), ruling Kerala (where I was born and raised) of about 35 million, *alternately* since 1957 – Communist party attained power through ballots for the first time in the world, in a significant population of a country, in 1957 in Kerala, forty years after Lenin seized power in Russia. (Communists ruled much larger W. Bengal with a population of about 90 million, from 1977 to 2011 straight, not alternately, but without the progress Kerala achieved.) We now know what happened to Salvador Allende in 1973!

Kerala's progress has later been extended to the neighboring Tamil Nadu with about 68 million, without the influence of communists, and largely by copying the *Kerala model*; I wish all of India copied the *Kerala model,* which is not impractical. (One report showed infant mortality in Kerala is at par with that of the U.S. with less than 10% of *Per capita* Purchasing Power!) "Kerala has a Human Development Index of 0.79 which is 'high' (Norway: 0.96, highest; USA: 0.93; Saudi Arabia: 0.85; Cuba: 0.78; China:

0.76; India, as a whole: 0.65), and the highest in India. Kerala is also highest in literacy among all Indian states at 96.2% and a female life expectancy of 79 years [male 73.5], which is among the highest in the country"- *Wikipedia*]

The prevailing wage for regular manual laborers in Kerala has been comparable to that of what California's Fast-Food workers are scheduled to get from April 2024, $20/hour. And Kerala has been a magnet for such workers from other parts of India, as far away as from Bihar and W. Bengal, where the wages for regular laborers have been comparable to the *pathetic American Minimum Wage,* as of 2023!

The saddest aspect of poverty in India and other poor countries is that the well-off consider the poor 'not fully' human. Only the problems of the well-off are considered genuine national problems!

Furthermore, most pundits who write about India claim the 400 million "middle class" folks in India as a mark of progress. But I would argue they attained that "middle class life" by exploiting the poor who toil hard in a variety of manual labor at *too low* wages, including as servants at middle class homes.

But through democratic means, in the 20th century America with the ***"New Deal" and the "War on Poverty," great strides in poverty alleviation have been made***; (the former more for whites than for others, but the latter was about universal). The same has been achieved even more equitably in *Scandinavia* and much of (Western) Europe, *through* democratic means.

The New Deal was the inspiration for President <u>Lyndon B. Johnson's Great Society</u> in the 1960s: Johnson (on right) was elected to Congress in 1938.

Indeed, Britain's Tony Benn saw socialism as the "<u>culmination of democratization</u>." Alternatively, I would say, **"democracy is 'incomplete' without socialism, and that socialism is 'incomplete' without democracy."** (I would add **this dictum has been reinforced, if not proved by FDR with the New Deal and Mikhail Gorbachev with Perestroika and Glasnost.**) Amartya Sen, a Nobel Laureate in Economics (1998) observed similarly that democracy can function as an antidote to famine and undue suffering of the poor. Indeed, India, the country now with the largest population in the world started displaying this phenomenon, which has been (very) gradually evolved, but large sections of India still remain "dirt poor."

After Stalin's brutal suppression of opposition with far too numerous executions of his mostly imagined and some real (such as Leon Trotsky) opponents, Nikita Khrushchev first and finally, Mikhail Gorbachev with "*perestroika* and *glasnost*" tried to incorporate a good deal of democracy into a seasoned soviet socialism. Unfortunately, ***that endeavor backfired crushing a sprouting democracy, as well as their seasoned socialism, owing partly to Boris Yeltsin's incompetence, inebriation and disengagement and to Vladimir Putin's ruthless oppression of his opponents***.

Vladimir Putin claimed that the dissolution of the Soviet Union was the greatest tragedy of [the latter half of] the 20th century. But I would argue the ouster of Gorbachev, *TIME* magazine's "Man of the Decade," probably would have been a more appropriate designation as *among* the greatest tragedies of the latter half of the 20th century. But the Khmer Rouge regime under Pol Pot, and the Kim dynasty in North Korea could be viewed as far worse, comparable to the *Holocaust*.

In 2003, while at war, Bush cut long-term capital gains-tax to just 15%. President Obama struggled to raise that rate to 20% (but effectively to 23.8%, with 3.8% Medicare tax) from 15%, which became effective in 2013. Both capital gains income and hedge-fund managing commissions, etc. are still taxed at 23.8%.

George H.W. Bush and Bill Clinton encountered substantial criticisms, for their moderate tax-hikes; Barack Obama also endured constant criticism and resistance from the Republicans. ***Obama, with the perennial support of Fed-chairman Ben Bernanke***, nevertheless ***managed to rescue the economy*** from the Great Recession. And the economy ***did not slip into another Great Depression***, thanks to Ben Bernanke, Hank Paulson, as well as George W. Bush (for accepting their advice), besides Obama.

The Republican party, under the leadership of Abraham Lincoln, fought the costliest civil war in history, wounding, literally and figuratively, most white families of America, essentially to end slavery!

But in the 20th (and 21st) centuries the (same) Republican party vehemently resisted, and continues to resist funding of Social Security, Medicare, Medicaid and lately Obamacare.

Nevertheless, **President Eisenhower wrote** in a private letter, **"Should any party attempt to abolish social security** [etc.], **you would not hear of that party again in our political history.** There is a tiny splinter group of course, that believes you can do these things ... Their number is negligible and they are stupid." **But in this Reagan era, their number is neither negligible nor are they "stupid.**

The Forgotten Mesmerizing Power of Certain Rare Leaders' Charisma

Leaders with enormous charisma as well as eloquence can get the masses do unbelievable things, an un/underappreciated reality, *rather a forgotten fact.*

  (*Donald Trump may be a good example among the living* – see his decisive influence in electing Mike Johnson as Speaker as well as *the huge majorities he captured in the 2024 Republican Primary elections, while Adolf Hitler is among the recent past, I think.*) But Trump, a certified "inept" leader, an "f*ing idiot," unlike Hitler, had little interest in governing as President, or helping, or (badly) hurting anyone other than *promoting* himself, with a never-ending quest to tell himself and the world, he's the "greatest," ever walked on American soil, in any and every respect! *Such a posture seems to leave the boundaries of sanity*, which makes it difficult to see much less accept his "greatness" – his reckless treatment and retention of the classified documents and his lawyers' inability to effectively counsel him hardly stand to reason, or normal behavior. Then again, the intensity of Hitler's antisemitic rage and his reckless invasion of the Soviet Union spilled over rational boundaries – **Nonetheless, Fidel Castro's judgments during his entire (almost) 50-year-rule was nearly flawless,** I think. See also, the swooning of Nikita Krushchev of Fidel, a lowly leader of a tiny Caribbean country which depended on the mighty Soviet Union to survive, let alone thrive as Cuba did, in over 100 pictures!

In a scientific paper, I wrote, "In a less dramatic way [compared with Joseph Goebbels adoring a 36-year-old Hitler], the American public was mesmerized by Ronald Reagan in the 1980s when they collectively perceived the immense contrast between him and Jimmy Carter. Reagan, like Franklin Roosevelt, offered simple solutions to complex problems, [and forcefully articulated them with their exceptional eloquence]; both displayed a total absence of ambiguity.

"These two titans could steer the middle-of-the-road American public decidedly to the left in the 1930s and 50 years later, decidedly to the right" (Alias AG. _Medical Hypotheses_ 2000;54(4):537-552; _p. 538_).

Indeed, in recent years, a widely respected presidential historian Jon Meacham has stated about the same, on _MSNBC Morning Joe_ and other programs, by dividing the past ninety years into the FDR era, and the Reagan era.

It is conceivable that post-Reagan Republicans, and many Democrats as well, are under Ronald Reagan's spell still, as the Garden-variety Republican, Dwight D. Eisenhower may have been under FDR's spell. Or it may well be that when something is too popular, people would rather go along with it than challenge it, not unlike the German public who passively colluded with the radical Nazis. And Reaganomics wins the day still.

And although the "FDR tax-hike" (the top-rate reaching an extremely high 94%, over on about $3 million in 2020 dollars) ended with the drastic "Reagan tax-cut" (to a top-rate of just 28%), **as much as Bill Clinton wanted to raise taxes of the rich and add some more "socialist programs,"** *including universal healthcare, he didn't have the charismatic clout, as FDR, or Reagan had, to raise the top income tax rate to any higher than 39.6%,* not quite 40%. And the Democrats suffered historic electoral defeat in 1994 midterm elections losing control of both chambers! He was rather "coerced" to announce, "The era of big government is over." And against his wishes, after vetoing twice before, he chose to sign the Republican 'welfare reform bill' in 1996, effectively kicking out far too many poor Americans of welfare.

The still popular "supply-side" economic theory, pushed during the Reagan administration had a lot to do with the rising inequality. Furthermore, *the supply-side theory was convincingly discredited* more recently with a *real life experiment in Kansas.* The Kansas Republican Sate-lawmakers over-rode the veto of Republican Gov. Sam Brownback who was hellbent on sticking to the supply-side theory.

The Guardian reports, citing Oxfam, by the end of 2016, just eight richest people in the world had as much wealth as the bottom half of the world's total 7.5 billion people! Lower rates of tax collection from the rich probably are the major factor for this (dangerous) inequality. And by 2017, the then richest, three Americans, Bill Gates, Jeff Bezos and Warren Buffett, had even more wealth than the bottom half of all Americans.

However, Warren Buffett has pledged 99% of his wealth to go to charity. His late wife and children have been fully supportive of his "super-generosity." He used to say he was good at making money but not good at distributing it, giving it away judiciously, as he always wanted to. (Bill Gates used to say, "in the end I will give it all away," before he started his foundation) Whereas, Bill Gates, along with his former wife, has been exceptionally good at it. Buffett saw this and decided to generously donate, unload much of his riches on to the Gates foundation. He has already donated $50.7 billion to the Gates

Foundation and to four foundations connected to his family, according to a Chronicle tally! Bill and Melinda French Gates have so far donated about $36 billion to their foundation (Bill Gates added another $20 billion to his pile of donation to their foundation in July 2022). They have pledged about 90% of their wealth to go to charity (How their foundation, which has been the **largest and most effective in world history**, would fare, with their divorce may be uncertain.) Elon Musk and Jeff Bezos haven't *yet donated much to charity, but Bezos's ex-wife has* indeed donated handsome amounts to charity, which she probably savors.

And just because many superrich in America over the past 100 years have been quite charitable, that can't obviate the misery of the less fortunate.

As the charitable donations of the presidential candidates reveal, charities' impetus varies widely:

	Income	(Year)	Charitable Donations as Percentage of Income
Mitt Romney:	$13.69 million	(2011)	29.4%
Barack Obama:	$790,000	(2011)	21.8%
Carly Fiorina:	$1.95 million	(2013)	13.4%
Hillary Clinton:	$27.9 million	(2014)	10.8%
Bernie Sanders	$205,300	(2014)	5.0%
Jeb Bush	$8.28 million	(2014)	3.7%
Ted Cruz	$2 million	(2010)	0.9%

Through progressive taxation-law, the government ought to step in and ease the misery of the less fortunate, by taxing the affluent at a modestly higher rate than in 2023, to spend on various safety-net programs such as food stamps, greater EITC, Welfare, Social Security, Medicaid and the Obamacare.

However, Alan Reynolds of the Cato Institute wrote, **"[The] topic of marginal tax rates became the central theme of a revolution in economic policy** [touted as Supply-side taxation theory, in that 'tax-cuts' for the rich would pay for itself, unleashing a miraculous growth] **that swept the globe.** ... By the end of [1980s], more than fifty nations had significantly reduced their highest marginal tax rates. **Neither Karl Marx nor John Maynard Keynes had so much influence** [as Ronald Reagan had] **on so many countries in so little time."**

But at this juncture, *rather than tax-cuts,* as the Republican majority did in 2017, *tax increases* on "top" incomes as well as levying modest annual taxes on estimated wealth are what's needed.

A big majority of Americans, including a not insignificant minority of the rich wants tax-hikes on the rich, as the inequality is so high, and most middle income and poor Americans struggle to make ends meet – There are far too many examples for poorer Americans as well as billions of less well-off elsewhere struggle to make ends meet.

A telling example is how two middle class hard-working breadwinners in Milwaukee, WI, one white, the Newmans and the other black, the Stanleys depicted in *Frontline* when they lost their manufacturing jobs following the closure of their factories over thirty years ago.

Another example is the immense contrast in "total, net remunerations" between two janitors, one at *Kodak* in Rochester, NY about forty years ago compared with another janitor at *Apple,* now. What the janitor at *Apple, as among the most valuable two or three corporations in the world, as well as in history,* receives is about pittance compared with the janitor at *Kodak* received! (Kodak was a Dow 30 stock from 1930 until 2004. Kodak had to declare chapter 11 bankruptcy in 2012.) Such huge differences in remunerations is a reflection of how society in general views the "worth" of workers, which I would assert is a passively evolved phenomenon, with far-reaching negative impact on the society at large.

The Danger of Going to Extremes, Including in Taxation

We all have an inherent tendency to go to extremes, in accumulating wealth, and stuff which we may never even use like Imelda Marcos's shoe collection. Or in expanding a despot's empire as Alexander the Great and Genghis Khan did, or Napoleon and Hitler attempted but failed, by invading Russia. Or what Bush-Chaney did (with the advice of Henry Kissinger but against the advice of Bush_41's senior aides) by invading Iraq in 2003, which led to the creation of a most brutal ISIS/Daesh, all but destroying Syria. Barack Obama's inaction made the matter far worse, not unlike the creation of a far more brutal Marxist, Khmer Rouge regime in Cambodia, from the Vietnam war – Kissinger had a prominent, if not decisive role in this!

(And Kissinger could have prevented the Bangladesh/East Pakistan genocide of a million or more Bengalis in 1971, **if he had a conscience,** after escaping the Holocaust by fleeing Germany in 1938. "Kissinger sneered at people who 'bleed' for 'the dying Bengalis'," says his *Wikipedia* page! He had contemptuously remarked, Bangladesh would be an "international basket case," but the poverty rate in Bangladesh is now estimated to be much *lower* than that in Pakistan and probably less than that in India as well.)

As for the marginal tax rates in the U.S., in the early years of World War II, the top marginal tax rate went up, all in 2020 dollars, from 81% on over about $88 million in 1941 to 88% on over (just) 3.17 million in 1942, then to 94% on over about $3 million in 1944 (President Roosevelt indeed sought a 100% tax on over about $4 million - Bernie Sanders's 2016 tax plan only called for a top marginal tax rate of 54% on over $10 million, 'not 90% on most of what we make' - a CBS News reporter visibly cringed by hearing the [erroneous] 90% figure, as seen on television)

Or, the top marginal, federal individual income tax rate ought to go up to about **50% but only on, say, the top 0.1% household incomes from all sources. Long term capital gains, carried interest loophole, etc. should end at incomes over about $500K, for taxation**. (Some or far too many may not realize that up to the initial $500K "taxable income," these uber-rich would pay at the existing rates.)

Somehow, Sen. Bernie Sanders has an extremely powerful, erroneous image, when it comes to taxes and other social issues. And people *assume*, without having a clear grasp of them, his ideas are *radically socialist*. In fact, Bernie Sanders's 2016 tax plan was **FAR MORE MODEST than the taxes levied on the affluent during the ENTIRE eight years of EISENHOWER administration!** (I would ask the readers to verify this on available data by Googling, or other reliable literature search.) Sanders's 2016 tax plan can be used as a template, a good model to craft a modestly higher progressive taxation, far less taxing to the affluent than they paid prior to 1981.

President John F. Kennedy, a Democrat, sought to cut the marginal tax rates across the board, but the top rate was meant to come down only to 65%, from 91% to spur growth. **That tax-cut was opposed by conservatives of both parties in Congress,** who were worried about the possible accumulation of *national debt*. After the JFK assassination, President Lyndon B. Johnson (LBJ) *managed* to cut the top rate to 70% in 1964, not to 65%. - Prominent Republicans continue to cite the *JFK tax-cut model* as a justification to cut income taxes, evermore but factually erroneous.

It is important to note that among the Republicans who voted against the 1964 "JFK tax-cut" bill, pushed by LBJ, was Sen. Barry Goldwater (R-AZ), the principal leader of the modern conservative movement. I think **as for preserving the very high marginal tax rates, or drastic tax-cuts, for the rich**, there might have been little difference in the ideological sentiments between Presidents Eisenhower and Reagan; **but I wonder whether they were fully cognizant of the dramatic differences between their manifest taxation policies.**

In April 2012, on *"Morning Joe"* (an *MSNBC program*) they were seriously discussing the tax rates both Barack Obama and Mitt Romney paid for 2011. Their effective tax-rates were too low, **solely because** *they donated rather huge amounts* **to (legitimate) charities**. But the discussants were apparently oblivious to that fact!

Furthermore, Mitt Romney's 'taxable' income mostly came from 'capital-gains-like' incomes to be taxed mostly at 15%, not at the top rate of 35%. Still Romney chose to donate over 29% [!] to deserving charities, well above the 10% or so his Mormon Church may have required. Not a single Democrat came to his defense when he was mercilessly attacked for at the too-low rate he paid his federal income tax, while also criticizing the low federal income tax Obama paid. Compare that with Sen. John McCain's defense of then Senator Barack Obama in 2008 when a woman complained to him that Obama was an "Arab."

Even the 70% rate was too high on over such a low amount of about $1.6 million in 1964, which was reduced by inflation to about $610,000 by 1980, both in 2020 dollars. Entrepreneurs must have resented it because far too much of what they made went as federal income tax.

Then in California, Howard Jarvis in 1978 managed to pass the "Proposition 13," drastically cutting Real Estate taxes. That had a national impact. Even otherwise taxes in California were already high because Ronald Reagan as Governor *paradoxically raised* them to triple the state revenue in eight years! This incongruity in the apportionment of taxation is again a sign of our general lack of knowledge and interest in taxation and tax-rates.

And during the 1980 election season, when Reagan said he would cut taxes, raise the military budget and still balance the budget, based on the "supply-side" economic principles, George HW Bush (correctly) called it ***"Voodoo economics."*** Reagan's eloquence and charm muted such criticisms; he handily won the 1980 election, also because he picked GHW Bush as his Vice-Presidential running mate, unlike Hillary Clinton who neglected to ask Bernie Sanders to become her running mate in 2016 – too much hubris. And we ended up with Donald Trump with the associated baggage. His incredible popularity among the U.S. public can be compared only with that of Adolf Hitler among the recent political figures.

Until the Reagan tax-cut with the dangerous "over-simplification" of federal income tax rates of 1986, the bulk of federal income taxes fell on the "richest few-percenters." The 1986 tax-reform was an unadulterated but stealth-assault on the middle class, and the American Middle-Class lifestyle. Ironically, that middle class, instead of eschewing the Republican party, became tethered to them, based on social and cultural issues like gay-marriage and abortion, along with a *subdued* opposition to the growing influence of African Americans in the Democratic party! And Ronald Reagan is a universally admired figure, despite that I view him as among the bad U.S.

Presidents! Whereas, unlike many or most scholars, I view Bill Clinton as a great President still, even a notch higher than GHW Bush (Bush_41); Bush_43 was the worst among the post-war presidents, a notch lower than even Richard Nixon!

The problem with such a low top rate is that the bulk of the tax-revenue would come from middle-income taxpayers, a recipe for rapidly shrinking middle class and widening inequality. I would argue the revered phrase, "Lower the Rate and Broaden the Base" is plain horrible, an unmitigated assault on the middle class. The federal income tax on the lowest income people/households ought to be reduced to lower than 10%, around 5%. Their payroll tax also ought to be drastically reduced as well.

Most of us do not quite understand, as said above, how our income taxes are structured and work for us. As said above, Bruce Bartlett writes, "[Congress] had no idea how many tax loopholes there were or how much revenue they were costing the Treasury." If such loopholes, or "tax-expenditures" were completely eliminated the tax revenue can go up by about a third. But most loopholes have justifiable reasons, at least when they were initially enacted.

We tend to believe if (the federal individual income) taxes were cut we all would pay less, which hardly applies to *most*. **Only the rich would benefit from progressive (income) tax cuts**. The 2017 tax-cut law is no exception, though the "non-rich" also get some crumbs, from this tax-cut law, which are more illusory.

MOST of us would be HURT from (income) tax-cuts, in general owing to the loss of revenue, and consequent, eventual cuts in public spending. On the other hand, ***(federal income)***

TAX-HIKES usually mean adding one or more brackets at the top, as in 1990, 1993 and 2013, which **WOULD BENEFIT LOWER-INCOME groups far more from more liberal spending on safety-net programs, etc., but "the top earners" would be squeezed, who can easily afford it,** even if some in the upper middle class end up paying 'a few more dollars.' However, **this is not immediately apparent to get enough public support.** The **higher revenue** to the treasury **comes mostly,** if not entirely **from the high-income groups. We all, including many among the affluent would benefit from higher public spending, etc., such as from infrastructure improvements.** When there is more money to spend without borrowing more, the **debt-to-GDP ratio would remain tolerable at least, if not falls.** And the general confidence in the economy would improve, somewhat like in the *Clinton* as well as the *Eisenhower* years.

The Higher tax on high incomes hardly hurts the economy; it's just propaganda conveniently put out by the affluent. During **the entire eight, Eisenhower years, the top federal income tax rate was 91%,** *when the (white) middle class flourished and America was seen and felt by Americans as the richest country* on earth, and in history as well!

Wealth Tax

Senator Elizabeth Warren proposed a wealth tax of 2% on wealth over $50 million, and 3% on wealth over $1 billion, annually. I sense that it is a little too high, which may not last from probable, concerted, determined opposition, as the high federal income tax rates on the rich in the post-war years didn't. I hope I am wrong.

But *as said earlier, both large tax-hikes of the forties, largely if not entirely by FDR's huge persuasive power and the subsequent deep tax-cuts with Reagan's about equally strong persuasive power, might not have materialized absent of those two titans, an un/underappreciated fact with huge, far-reaching consequences.*

Furthermore, an inescapable fact is that the wealthy are as a group, not only just luckier than the poor and the less well-off but are also generally smarter. And smart people would find ways to raise their incomes and to accumulate wealth, compared with not so smart people. On the way, they tend to exploit the deficiencies in luck and smartness of the less well-off, which is what led to so much financial inequality.

And I would suggest *taxing the wealth more modestly, so that a small but appreciable minority of the wealthy*

would see that such a taxation is only fair, even necessary. It is not too difficult to calculate the approximate value of wealth for the prior year, and assess their tax, as Real Estate and Property Taxes are assessed.

(I would request the readers to review the sentiments of *The Abolitionists*, which were enhanced by their *Christian spirituality* but may not quite resonate with certain modern "*Evangelical sprit*," though that spirituality would fully resonate with Pope Francis's teachings, I believe.)

The inheritance tax could be gradually phased out with an annual wealth tax, which would be less burdensome to the wealthy than levying their descendants when they inherit the wealth. Besides, the eventual elimination of inheritance tax, the so-called "death-tax," could be a selling point. Further, the revenue from inheritance tax has also been shrinking.

Temporary wealth tax of 5% may be levied on top 0.001% wealth, to shrink the financial inequality when it is too high as it is today.

Drastic Top Marginal Rate-Reduction Could Lead to Rise in Financial Crimes

When the top marginal rate came down from 70% in 1980 to 28% in the tax reform of 1986, for many high income taxpayers, it was too tempting to bend the rules to make more, as they could keep 42% more of what they made (I would also say **this was the "unkindest cut," accelerating inequality, which spread to the rest of the world as pointed out by** _Alan Reynolds of the Cato Institute._)

Eventually, the bending of rules did morph into breaking laws. Michael Milken, a creative genius in finance, for example broke laws. He raked in $550 million in 1987 (over a billion in 2020 dollars). Subsequently, he received ten years in prison but served only two.

In the mid-2000s, with the Bush tax-cuts, though the top rate was still 35%, by the drastic cuts in long-term capital gains, and with the carried interest loophole, taxes on the highest incomes dropped to a low of 22% by 2005, **which was near 60% around 1945 (Fig. 1)**. White-collar crimes shot up again. US attorney Preet Bharara secured 85 straight convictions since 2009 by the middle of 2014 on insider trading cases!

One could compare the very low tax-rates on very high incomes, tempting tycoons to break laws, to too liberal prescriptions of oxycodone of late by unscrupulous drug-companies with too compliant physicians and the resultant very high death rates from opiate overdoses, which more recently have crossed 100K in the prior 12 months!

Burden of Payroll and Local Taxes on the Working Poor

Federal payroll tax is brutal on the working poor. Many of them may not even realize its gravity. Payroll tax burden proportionately diminishes as the income goes up to reach negligible levels in the, say top 0.5% or so income households, as there is a cap ($137,700, for 2020; $160,200 for 2023, and $168,600 for 2024) on it beyond which payroll tax isn't levied. ***Thus, payroll tax is unconscionably regressive***.

Medicare tax is levied on all incomes, *but at the same rate*. The reason for this incongruity between Medicare and Payroll taxes is because, without levying a lot more, Medicare would go bankrupt, but Social Security trust fund, which is dependent of Payroll tax, has a longer lifespan.

And low-income households are greatly burdened by them. Too many of them regularly pay exorbitant interest rates to payday lenders to stay afloat. (As the paradise papers show, some of the richest people *legally* participate in this racket of payday-lending to further fatten their net worth.)

Therefore, (federal) Payroll tax should be cut to get a modest relief for the working poor and the lower middle class. The payroll tax on about the first $15,000 should be cut to 1%, and the second $15,000 to 2%. If the employers also get a relief on their share of payroll tax, they might pay a higher wage to their low wage employees.

To make up for the shortfall, the cap on it needs to go up. Preferably, the cap could be lifted, but then to make it less unpalatable to the rich, to avoid being too radical, the payroll tax should again be cut to about 2% beyond say, around $300,000. This could extend the social security solvency as well. Many youngsters of today feel social security may not be there for them when they become eligible to collect it.

Conclusion

And as embedded in the title, remunerations each of us gets have only a minimal correlation to what we are worth, based on our skills and effort. And the multimillion dollar-incomes and the multibillion dollar-wealth many managed to get have little if any justification, regardless of their legality. But the society has no right to "confiscate" them. Nevertheless, the society has a right as well as the duty to tax them but preferably, not too drastically.

And a decent progressive taxation is fully justified. But very high taxes, as what existed during and after WW II, *during the entire Eisenhower years, with a top rate of 91% on over around $4 million in 2020 dollars* on the affluent are "drastic," which may not last owing to the pull of natural forces, *nor are they necessary.*

Unfortunately, from the beginning of the Reagan presidency, the taxes have been far less progressive through Bush_43's 2003 capital gain tax-cuts, with some respite during the Clinton administration and since 2013, until the 2017 tax-cuts.

The principal reason why it is a lot easier to cut taxes for the rich than to raise on them, who can easily afford to pay higher taxes, the potential beneficiaries of higher taxes on the rich, the poor, do not sense the "pain" of tax cuts for the rich, unlike when they need to pay higher prices for say, groceries.

And they're eager to complain about inflation but are indifferent to the tax-cuts for the rich, though the latter **HURTS THEM MOST!**

Further, far fewer would advocate cutting regressive taxes unlike the constant, vocal plea for cutting progressive taxes; the latter benefits the affluent, almost exclusively while hurting most of the rest.

Furthermore, there's a pervasive, CRUEL MYTH (see the modestly and vastly discordant remunerations section in the text) *that the affluent pay all the taxes, because they have "all" the incomes while the poor get all the freebees from the affluent's taxes.*

A modest annual wealth tax ought to be levied, even if it is a little less than what Sen. Elizabeth Warren suggested. With this annual wealth tax, the inheritance taxes could possibly be phased out, if programed well, a selling point.

Moderate tax-hikes on the top 0.1% incomes, NOT EVEN ON TOP 1%, to about 50% to spend on various public service and social safety-net programs are substantially beneficial to any society. And the misery of the least among us must and can be alleviated.

Preferably, there could also be two more higher rates of 40% and 45% in between 37% and 50%.

Then, yet another top tax-bracket of 60% on over $25 million and even 70% on over $50 million, either as a temporary (or permanent) levy could be considered.

Reminding the readers once again, the top rate of 70% WAS ON OVER around $1 MILLION in 2020 dollars between 1965 and 1981. This would bring in hundreds of billions in additional revenue. And it could substantially reduce the budget deficit, and debt as well, and function as a brake on the rising financial inequality, which is necessary.

Robert Reich proposed a 70% top tax-rate on over $15 million incomes in 2011. Unfortunately, few Democrats supported that "modest proposal."

Paul Krugman, a Nobel Laureate (sole winner, Economics, 2008), among others, concludes the maximum tax revenue would be collected at around 73% on top incomes. Unfortunately, Krugman's image among the influential is not too unlike that of Bernie Sanders, largely negative. And they listen to him with a good initial dose of skepticism. He is a prolific writer. His 2012 book, *'End This Depression Now'* was discussed at length on Bill Moyers & Co (on Jan 11, 2013); listening to it is immensely informative.

Further, as others have suggested, a minuscule taxation on Wall Street transactions, to go up gradually to reach the European level is necessary, to benefit *investors* as opposed to "day-traders" and computer-based back-and-forth traders in lightning speed, which has little social value. Jesse Eisinger of *ProPublica* had an excellent article (2008) in the now defunct *Portfolio.com*. Eisinger writes, "On the New York Stock Exchange, turnover hit a high of 143% in 1928. Then turnover plummeted, staying below 20% from 1938, all the way to 1975. Since then, ... it rose to 59% in 1990 and to [215%] in 2007. Hedge funds account for much of this.... The [socially unimportant if not useless] market hyperactivity has been so enduring that hardly anyone notices, but the fact remains: **The long-term investor is extinct**[!]" (portfolio.com Sep. 18, 2008).

Gradually rising gasoline and diesel tax, a justifiable flat tax, to reach the European level in eight-to-ten years is also necessary, for the sake of our planet and for infrastructure repair and development. Perhaps, the fuel tax ought to be reserved for improvement and expansion of mass transit system.

Autobiographical information and some other matters

The details of my autobiographical account may be irrelevant to many readers and may be disregarded, what I posted below in small letters, along with other matters, the latter may or may not be relevant to the readers:

I am a retired Indian American psychiatrist, arrived in the USA in 1971. I have over fourteen, (only but) mostly single-author publications to my credit, including a short one in *The Lancet* – "Androgen-Dysgenesis: A Predisposing Factor in Schizophrenia?" (1972), which is more relevant now, with the discovery of neuroactive *sex-steroids* in the brain than in the 1970s when some complex combination of hyper as well as hypoactivity in the dopamine system in critical brain sites was seen as *the* determinant of schizophrenic psychopathology.

I sensed schizophrenia more as a *quantitative* variation from a "mean normal" psyche rather than as a *qualitative* variation. Behavioral scientists by and large, however, view schizophrenia more as a qualitative variation with hallucinations and delusions, so do the educated lay public. Genetic studies of the recent past, however, seem to cast doubts on a too narrower view of schizophrenic psychopathology, to confine the search in the dopamine system. Besides, neuroactive steroids influence the "dopamine system," as well as other neurotransmitters in a variety of ways.

I have been suffering from an enduring *depression*, which was mixed with an underlying *hypomania*, so to speak, almost all my life, which I suspected could also be a case of *dormant* schizophrenia. But this dormant schizophrenia helped me, I believe to develop a better insight into the psychopathology of schizophrenia. I had a fairly typical migraine with aura, in the form of scotoma, since age 15.

(Since 1965, I have been taking smaller doses of amitriptyline, works as a prophylactic to migraine, and other antidepressants [higher doses induced anxiety, becoming tongue-tied while speaking], as well as a tiny dose of a long-acting benzodiazepine, like Valium, just 1 mg daily lately; both of which have been substantially beneficial, though medication has its limitations - Until 1971, I took 15 mg of phenobarbital, when I needed to speak to an audience, which eased my stage fright.

A prominent *Ayurvedic* physician in Kerala treated me in 1952, for my migraine with a medicated oil to be applied on the scalp, along with some other Ayurvedic medicines including a purgative. He strongly advised me against engaging in both mental and physical heavy work. I took it to heart, "forcing" myself to be lazy, without sensing that I was already habitually lazy, and becoming still lazier ever since. But my migraine disappeared except once when I was '*burning midnight oil*' while preparing for a midterm college examination/test. Some readers may be interested in this elaboration: Before I ever experienced my migraine "attacks," if I took a nap during the daytime, I sensed unusual nausea after I woke up. I then automatically [without any training] and forcefully would exhale through my nose, which was audible to others. Eventually, the nausea would go away, and I would feel normal. Amitriptyline also had relieved my nausea, if I occasionally experienced it, even now. The medicated oil when applied to the scalp had also relieved my nausea-like sensation, in addition to relieving my migraine, though not instantly.)

Since around age 16, nevertheless, I developed an extraordinary confidence in my intuitive reasoning ability – my hypomania may have enhanced this confidence. Periodically, however, the recognition of that dormant schizophrenia (schizotypy) challenged that confidence. I have also been quite low in likeability. Not infrequently, I tend to bring out the worst instincts in people I interact with (as confirmed by my wife, since 1969), though rather rarely, people do appreciate me, very much so, nonetheless – Schizotypy tends to diminish likeability, while hypomania enhances it. I had very few if any close friends. And I tend to bore people too often. And when I begin to voice an opinion, the listeners often would look for ways to refute me, as if I had no right to opine on anything, unless I am (very rarely) unusually articulate.

Though many experts in behavioral science have trashed my theory on the schizophrenic psychopathology, late Prof. George Ulett, MD, PhD (who lived until 97), of the University of Missouri commented (Nov. 3, 1999), on my 12,000-word-manuscript, "I found your excellent paper to be most interesting.... Your hypothesis has importance not only for schizophrenia but also for greater understanding of mental processes and dreaming." I published that paper in *Medical Hypotheses*, 2000;54(4):537-552.

I published another single-author, short paper in *The New Eng. J. Medicine* (1985), on the unique value of sugar as the *cheapest* source of (protein-sparing) calories (the caloric yield per hectare for sugarcane is several fold greater than that for rice, wheat or corn) which can be stored and transported without getting spoiled, indefinitely, as a cheap source of calories particularly in famine-stricken areas (since sugar *WAS* considered a luxury food item for centuries, it is quite difficult to view sugar as a

CHEAP article of food) - About 20% of the calories of "high

protein" nutritional supplements, such as *Ensure* or *Boost*, has been from sugar, including "Africa's miracle food" *Plumpy'nut,* despite a popular notion that sugar is "toxic" – 93-year-old Warren Buffett, in good physical and mental health, consumes some five cans or equivalent of *regular cherry-coke* (700 Cal.) daily! In 2015, Buffett told *Fortune* he was "one-quarter Coca-Cola."

When caloric intake is limited, tissue protein would be robbed to maintain blood sugar and to synthesize peptides for immune functions, etc. So, adequate intake of, **not excess**, calories are necessary. Increased protein intake under limited caloric intake won't help much. In 1974, a paper in *The Lancet*, entitled, "*The Great Protein Fiasco*" was quite critical of the public's obsession with protein.

I wish, in famine relief camps, 10-30% of the calories the residents are fed were from sugar, say as soda,

(about U.S. 18.00 cents/1,800 Calories) to reduce the cost, also to limit contamination.

I have also made some thirty (mostly, poster) presentations at various medical conferences, the abstracts of them have been published in different medical journals.

Owing to a series of misfortunes, along with faulty judgments on my part, I couldn't get a stable academic appointment in any American universities, though I had an *Emeritus Professor* (*biochemistry*) status in an Indian (Amrita, Kochi) University – I have a doctoral degree in biochemistry in the Faculty of Medicine from the University of Kerala, 1970, secured only with my second attempt.

I may add, I haven't been that good a student. I was about average, throughout. I am a very slow reader. I had repeated first & third grades, partly because of attendance deficiency; I was away. I passed my Psychiatry boards in 1979, only at the *fifth* attempt; I took MRC-Psych examination but couldn't make it. For SSLC (Secondary School Leaving Certificate, 1953), however, my rank was 6th of 135 students; and I was among the top third for MBBS (equal to MD/DO, in the U.S.).

I have also published several articles in Indian lay press on how to revise the Indian Constitution from a dangerously unstable Parliamentary system to a *more* stable Presidential system as in the U.S., but substantially modified – Prime Minister's power is too elastic, from that of a mere puppet if their parliamentary majority is precarious, to that of a dictator if their parliamentary majority is comfortable as well as in a *strong* personality, when the Prime Minister controls both the executive and the legislative branches of the state. (The President controls only the "Executive" branch.)

Both Jawaharlal Nehru and Indira Gandhi had, and used dictatorial powers, so has Narendra Modi, but in between there were Prime Ministers who hardly ruled, or lasted any significant length in office.

The omnipotent Congress party, of the 20th century, has all but shrunk to extinction, largely because, I think Rahul Gandhi, Indira Gandhi's grandson is a *weak* leader; ***a "substitute" leader outside the Nehru family turned out to be unacceptable to the rank-and-file Congress party members.*** Curiously, Sanjay Gandhi was the heir apparent to Indira Gandhi when he was living but his widow and son are regular members of the *Bharatiya Janata Party (BJP)*, no less!

But in an "immature" democracy, the President could abuse their power, as Vladimir Putin does. Then again, the title could have less relevance, dependent on the strength of the leader's personality, charisma and eloquence. Adolf Hitler secured absolute power, even stronger than that of most monarchs, in a matter of months, as Prime Minister equivalent, Chancellor.

Furthermore, in one of the most mature democracies, USA, Donald Trump almost assumed dictatorial powers! ***Even over three years after leaving his presidency, his hold on the Republican legislature is phenomenal!*** My reading is that it was a reflection of his amazingly powerful personality and charisma, *albeit his mind is disordered,* which makes it all the more difficult for the majority to see him that charismatic –

Michael Cohen, after he split with Trump, writes in his book, *Disloyal,* 2020, Pp., 42-43: "*I confess I never really did understand why pleasing Trump meant so much to me,* and others. To this day I don't have the full answer. *In a matter of couple of months, I had started under the spell of Donald Trump*. ... It seemed to them [my wife and children] that I wouldn't listen to anyone ... *as I gradually gave up control of my mind to Trump.*"

Trump's silent influence on the populace who identify as Republican is amazingly *strong* and unprecedented! Trump's detractors ridicule him, mercilessly so, nonetheless, as he habitually presents himself in the light of that disordered mind, but his followers (disciples, so to speak) ignored or couldn't recognize that disorder – I may be wrong, but my diagnosis is that he has a very rare, *unique case of chronic hypomania but without the inevitable depressive swings, in a narcissistic personality*.

Nassir Ghaemi, a prominent Iranian American psychiatrist writes in his book on leaders' characteristics, *"Depression makes leaders more realistic and empathic* (Trump is exhibit 'A' who is devoid of empathy, and he refuses to accept reality – he insists he won the November 2020 election, which is echoed by an amazing number of his ardent followers [!],) while mania makes them more creative and resilient." - Trump's prescriptions for Covid, by attacking the virus with Lysol, etc. could also be viewed as examples of his creative brainstorms but few would accept such an argument other than seeing it as purely irrational.

In 1960, I wrote a poem, the only poem I have written, penning down the idea I developed a few years earlier, in which I alluded to the natural "buffering" mechanism whereby any changes to a *'system in equilibrium'*, are often accompanied by a natural canceling/depleting out mechanism inherently built into it, say as scientific progress coinciding with scientific destruction. Even religious belief systems tend to reverse their intended impacts – Conception of *sin* in Christianity, unlike the prescriptions for good and bad deeds in the Old Testament, is *too slippery*. Christ pardoned the mythical prostitute, Mary Magdalene who eventually became his disciple, no less. At the same time, he told a rich young man who adhered to all the ten commandments about strictly, to do more, a lot more by renouncing *all, not half or a sizeable portion of* his assets. Christ was too liberal, completely forgiving of the sinners on the one hand, as he did with the thief on his right side (St. Dismas) while he was crucified, but his demands on the righteous were too burdensome, completely divorced from his Jewish faith and its prescriptions! This illustrates the built-in, buffering mechanism even in the prescriptions of religious teachings.

Many scholars contend that religion is the root of all/most evils. Hindus and Muslims, besides living peacefully side-by-side for centuries, but have occasionally fought and killed each other in India, which was profound during the Partition in 1947. But Sunni and Shia Muslims have also killed each other. ISIS has been more brutal to fellow Muslims. Catholics and Protestants carried out a 30-year bloody civil war in Northern Ireland. (There have been other Christian denominations that argued and fought with each other, over the centuries) Throughout human history people fought and killed each other, which actually has been the "other side" of human tendency to congregate and enjoy each other's company on the one hand, but then they tend to repel from one another, for one or another reason and fight and kill each other. Both instincts are natural, an example of the buffering mechanism.

I may quote a couple of lines from that poem: "... I call life a pendulum, obeying the law; Happiness and sorrow are the pendulous swings. By life, excited the pendulum; By this, a solution is aspired to. Science, Philosophy, Religion, will you solve? Answer me, answer me...."

Another good example is the value and convenience of plastic in everyday life, which is coming with its nuisance in the ocean and elsewhere as well as a more dangerous contamination of microplastic and probably still more dangerous nanoparticles we consume regularly, perhaps!

----

www.ingramcontent.com/pod-product-compliance
Lightning Source LLC
Chambersburg PA
CBHW032102020426
42335CB00011B/462